FAVORITE
Classics For Piano

Volume IV
Advanced

World-Famous Piano Solos
and Arrangements of Classical Melodies

Music selected and edited by Dale Tucker
Special arrangements written by Robert Schultz
Orchestrated accompaniment CD created by Andy Selby
Art design by Carmen Fortunato

WARNER BROS. PUBLICATIONS - THE GLOBAL LEADER IN PRINT
USA: 15800 NW 48th Avenue, Miami, FL 33014

WARNER/CHAPPELL MUSIC

CANADA • SCANDINAVIA • AUSTRALIA

Carisch
NUOVA CARISCH

ITALY • SPAIN • FRANCE

IMP
INTERNATIONAL MUSIC PUBLICATIONS LIMITED

ENGLAND • GERMANY • DENMARK

PREFACE

As with the first three books in this series, we feature world-renowned classical favorites by many composers from many countries. Included are original piano solos as well as arrangements and transcriptions of famous instrumental and orchestral works, all selected with the advanced pianist in mind. The CD provides orchestrated accompaniments to play along with, making you the soloist with your own in-house orchestra. We are sure this volume will provide years of pleasure to you and all who hear you play.

C O N T E N T S

CANON IN D

JOHANN PACHELBEL
Transcribed for Piano by ROBERT SCHULTZ

Canon in D - 10 - 1

Canon in D - 10 - 2

6

Canon in D - 10 - 3

Canon in D - 10 - 4

8

Canon in D - 10 - 6

Canon in D

10

Ped. ✳   Ped. ✳   *pedal simile*

p

f

- 10 - 7

Canon in

Canon in D - 10 - 10

MEDITATION
(from the opera *Thaïs*)

JULES MASSENET
Transcribed for Piano by ROBERT SCHULTZ

Meditation - 5 - 1

Meditation - 5 - 2

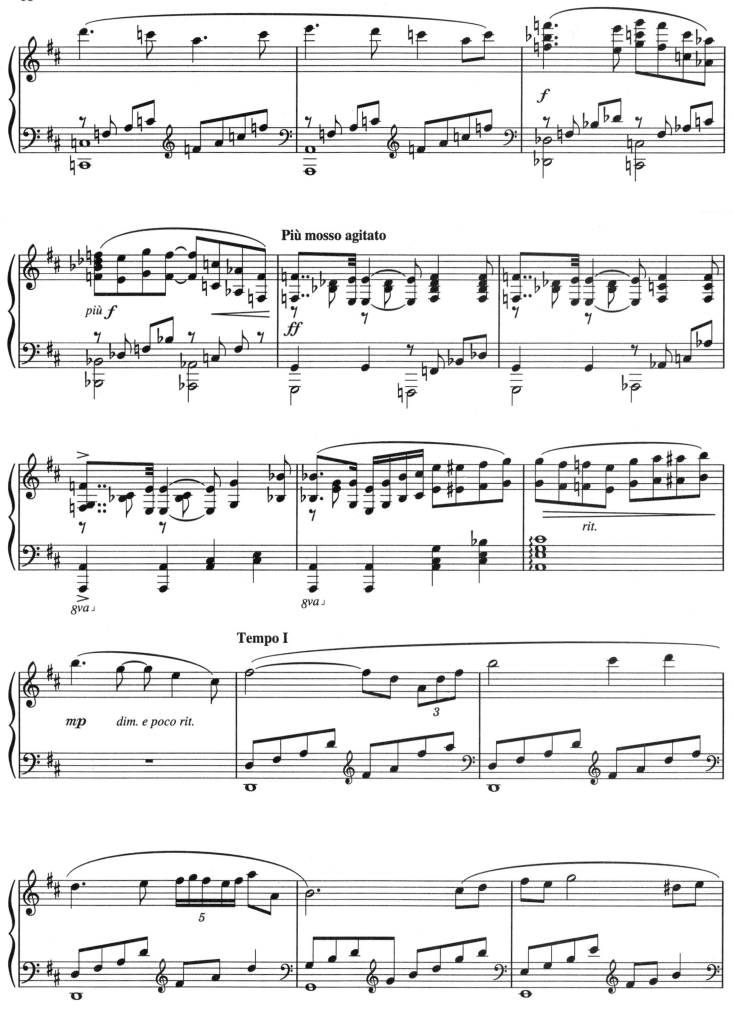

Meditation - 5 - 4

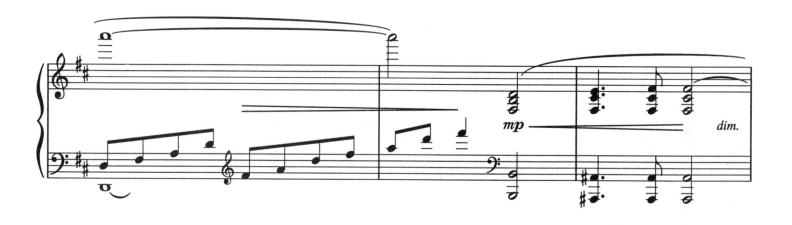

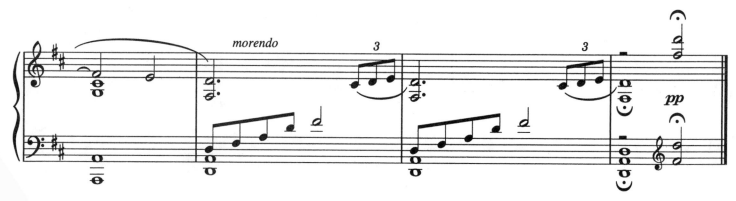

PRELUDE
Opus 28, No. 20

FREDERIC CHOPIN

EIGHTEENTH VARIATION
(from *Rhapsodie on a Theme of Paganini*)

SERGEI RACHMANINOFF
Adapted for Piano Solo by HERMENE W. EICHORN

Andante cantabile

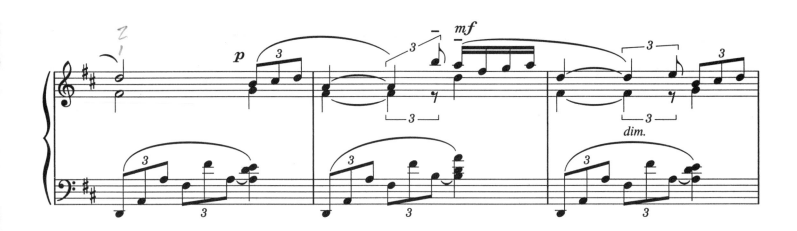

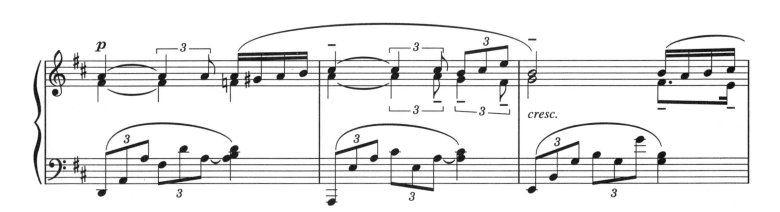

Eighteenth Variation - 4 - 1

Eighteenth Variation - 4 - 4

THE "MINUTE WALTZ"
Opus 64, No. 1

FREDERIC CHOPIN

26

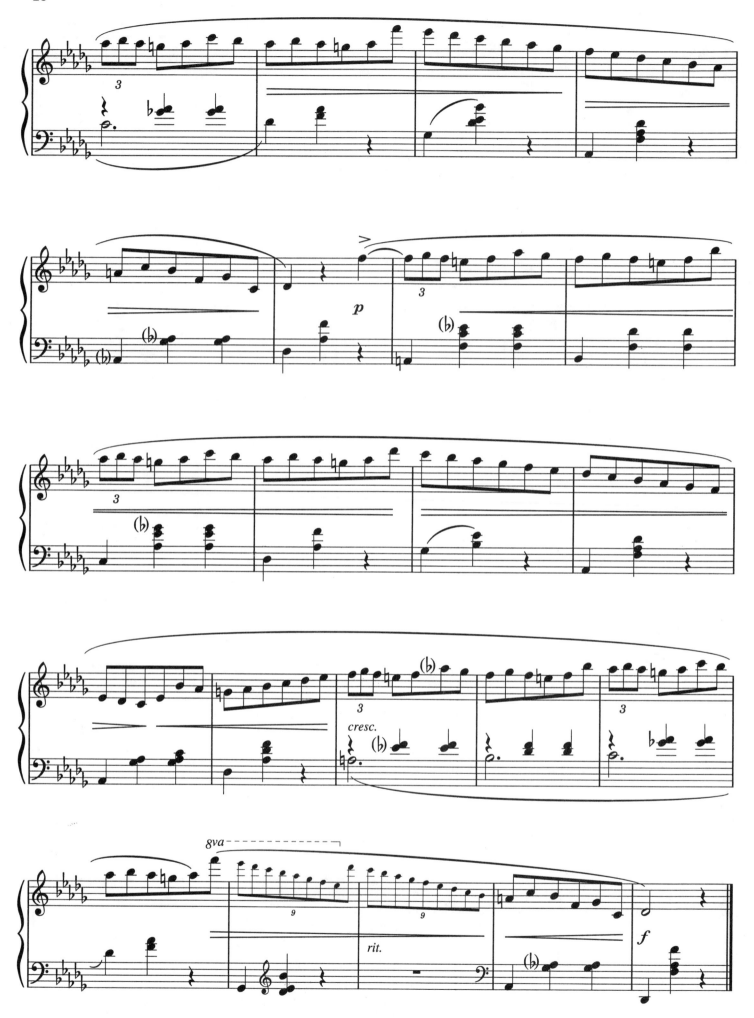

HUNGARIAN DANCE NO. 5

JOHANNES BRAHMS

Hungarian Dance No. 5 - 3 - 2

Hungarian Dance No. 5 - 3 - 3

THE SWAN
(from *Carnival of the Animals*)

CAMILLE SAINT-SAËNS
Transcribed for Piano by ROBERT SCHULTZ

The Swan - 3 - 1

THE PATHETIQUE SONATA
Opus 13
(First Movement)

LUDWIG VAN BEETHOVEN

Allegro di molto e con brio

to Monsieur A. Arensky

PRELUDE IN C SHARP MINOR
Opus 3, No. 2

SERGEI RACHMANINOFF

Tempo primo